How To Make Money Online

Various ways to make money online without spending a dime

Isah Abdulwali Garba

DEDICATION

This book is dedicated to my parents Mr./Mrs. Garba Omeji and to my friends and relations and to those who have not found my contents yet.

CONTENTS

INTRODUCTION

What Is Internet Marketing?

Affiliate Marketing

Article Marketing

Email Marketing

Blog Marketing

Pay-per-click or PPC

Search Engine Optimization

Pop-Up Ads

Banner Ads

Social Media Marketing

Mobile Marketing

Introduction

Welcome to the universe of Web Advertising! This guide is planned particularly for the individuals who are new to the universe of web promoting... or IM as some might call it. With this aid, you will be acquainted with the essential strategies of this industry and furthermore to a lot better quality and more complicated frameworks of web showcasing. Nonetheless, prior to pursuing this aide, open your brain to the colossal potential outcomes of the advertising scene. Sooner or later, you might discover a portion of the things that will be examined excessively confounded for you to start with. Nonetheless, these points and bits of information will the entire get sorted out and will additionally assist you with grasping this precise approach to advertising. Over the long haul, this will ensure your general progress in this excursion. Simply attempt to consider this little aid a lot of unique pieces which will ultimately interface with give you a total picture eventually. Sounds invigorating? Amazing! How about we start.

What Is Web Showcasing? Web showcasing is presently called by countless different names - e-advertising, web promoting, I-promoting, computerized promoting, web-based promoting and so forth. In any case, in straightforward language, it very well may be characterized as the showcasing of one's items or administrations that a business or individual proposes using the web. This sort of promotion incorporates an exceptionally wide region of the subject as it likewise incorporates many kinds of showcasing procedures like email and remote media showcasing. Under this overall extent of web showcasing likewise falls the parts of ECRM or electronic client relationship the board and computerized client information. For what reason is the web showcasing a major benefit to numerous organizations? The internet has given us numerous interesting and fundamental advantages. This innovation empowered the whole world to be associated with one another in practically no time. As far as online organizations, the web has given a worldwide gateway in which labor and products can be sold and purchased by nearly anybody and in any region of the planet. With web promoting, a wide range of organizations have participated in the lower expenses of data dispersal and ads. The web's intelligent nature has helped business advertising through moment reactions and its capacity to evoke them in the 6 quickest ways imaginable. Besides, web showcasing has integrated every one of the parts of inventiveness, detail, commercial, deals and item advancement. With its reasonable expense, web promoting has likewise empowered organizations to save money on their method for arriving at their objective market or crowd. Through a little part of the expense of customary notices, organizations can additionally permit their clients to direct research and in the long run buy their items in the most helpful manner. This likewise makes them more interesting to their clients since they can bring about an extremely limited capacity to focus time. Web promoting has likewise permitted these organizations to quantify their measurements in a much simpler and reasonable manner. Since practically every one of the parts of this showcasing type can be estimated, tried and followed using promotion servers, publicists can without much of a stretch use and notice their information regarding which promotions harvest the most client perspectives or buys. Along these lines, online organizations will actually want to figure out which of their promoting messages are more interesting to their objective clients. The consequences of every one of their missions can be followed immediately since this promoting drive just requires a client to tap the promotions, visit a specific site or play out an ideal activity like finishing up a structure or buying an item or administration. Presently as a fledgling in the realm of web showcasing, you will be liable for the undertaking of getting expected clients by giving them the administrations or the organization that suits their necessities or inclinations in different web scenes. You will assist these clients with finding 7 the item that they are searching for. The objectives are individuals who have PCs with web access. Business visionaries like you can visit your web-based store whenever. Buyers can likewise do the equivalent at whatever point they need. The fate of the internet is so brilliant with its projected web-based purchaser traffic coming to practically 60% and more than 80% of these clients shopping on the web. Thus, assuming still up in the air to make it fruitful for you, you may simply wind-up partaking in the advantages of having a web-based business that will give you more benefit over the long haul. So, web showcasing brings you many benefits of causing negligible costs in firing up your business including less expensive publicizing choices, a worldwide commercial center, turning into your own chief, advancing stuff that you are energetic about and benefitting from these interests en route. Sounds astonishing, right? However, there are many advantages from web advertising, it accompanies its own portion of dangers and ventures. You should comprehend that this cycle won't allow you to make large chunks of change rapidly. Your time, determination, tirelessness and energy for learning more are vital in your progress in web advertising. The individuals who imagine that this is an easy money scam will undoubtedly be frustrated. However numerous organizations have become very fruitful, you will track down that the people who have bombed in this adventure have basically wished to turn out to be for the time being moguls. The real factors of an actual business are as yet pertinent to your internet-based store, including charge installments, client administrations and in any event, recruiting representatives. 8 Besides, you must realize that beginning an internet-based business isn't free. There are costs that might be not as much as what will be utilized in building an actual business, however you will in any case need to dish out for website composition, programming, facilitating, spaces and publicizing costs. One more truth of having an internet-based business is web page free time. Indeed, your site might go down because of specialized hardships or errors, and this will presumably bring a ton of disappointment on your part as well as on the clients' end. Each and every moment or second that your site is inaccessible to guests and possible clients, you will lose cash. You should be ready for this. Moreover, you can't simply depend on a specific framework and have it run on autopilot to create benefits. Innovation changes and the business develops quickly, making any "autopilot framework" that should create cash a total falsehood. A showcasing strategy that worked for somebody in the past may not work for you by any means from now on. Hence, it is vital to keep yourself refreshed with new innovations and advertising patterns. Rivalry will continuously be near so on the off chance that you don't keep yourself informed and you don't really buckle down, you won't captivate everyone. You need to have an effect! Really buckle down since, in such a case that not, you should rest assured that one of your rivals is out there doing as such. Plus, in the event that you maintain that your business should be a drawn-out speculation, your most memorable benefits ought to return to your site's administrations and promoting endeavors. Boost your benefits and don't simply cash out your most memorable income. It will likewise be useful to find out about tax collection and other related regulations that influence this industry. Along these lines, you understand what your duty and lawful 9 benefits are once you set up your business. This will likewise help in safeguarding your resources; accordingly, it ought to never be neglected. In light of this multitude of real factors, you should still be up in the air to hang out in this industry. Web showcasing isn't for the individual who likes straightforward schedules. You ought to be adaptable in learning new methodologies and patterns to stay aware of your opposition. Since it is now so obvious what web showcasing is and every one of the great and awful that accompanies it, you will presently gain proficiency with the advertising techniques that internet-based organizations have been involving to advance their administrations and items to the worldwide commercial center. The accompanying techniques that will be talked about additional in the following couple of sections are: Subsidiary advertising Article showcasing Email promoting Website showcasing Pay per click advertisements or PPC Site design improvement or Web optimization Spring up advertisements Pennant promotions virtual entertainment showcasing Portable showcasing 10 These web showcasing strategies are not equivalent by any means. Every one of them has systems to arrive at an objective market and will deliver fluctuating outcomes in view of your objective, showcasing pitch and relationship with your client. Whether you will showcase your own site or decide to engage in subsidiary promoting, you are undoubtedly going to utilize several of these strategies at different times. Keep in mind, what you procure in this industry is consistently proportionate to all the work and time you have put resources into fostering your site. Presently we should continue with the delicious piece of this subject. In the following couple of pages, you will gain proficiency with every one of the web advertising techniques referenced previously. You will get to understand what they are, what they do, how they work and why they are powerful.

What Is Internet Marketing-

Web Advertising is a web-based practice wherein a business remunerates a partner for the guests or clients got by his advertising endeavors. The prizes are either money or gifts and are given for either a proposition culmination or site reference. In this cycle, there are four players - the trader, organization, distributor and client. As of late, this market has developed complex with the optional players like subsidiary administration organizations, outsider sellers (specific) and super-members. It works by basically utilizing the partner's site to direct people to the vendor's own website or to permit guests to be sent to the dealer's fundamental page. 11 Fundamentally, this is additionally the very thing that we can call income dividing among the internet-based dealers and online members. The remuneration given to the members really rely on the number of clients that snaps, deals or enrollments were made on the shipper's site through their own. Member promoting empowers the computerization of the publicizing processes and the installment for wanted activities. Dealers have favored this web showcasing technique since it is a "pay per execution" model, where they cause no costs for promoting their items except if the subsidiary delivers the outcomes they need. Partner showcasing can likewise be interpreted as a kind of business relationship where you, as a subsidiary, advance a dealer's administration which is not quite the same as yours. This implies that you don't have to have your own item to wander into subsidiary promotion. You just have to advance your business supplier's administrations and items. This is the way it works - you want to have a page that contains a connection that guides your clients or guests to the primary page or online store of the dealer. At the point when one of your webpage guests taps on that connection and buys something from the trader's site, you will get a kind of commission or a reference charge. This way you are the one directing people to your shipper's site through your own page. The trader will pay you at whatever point a guest from your site purchases something or pursues something on their site. A unique partner connect is doled out to your page, making it simple for the trader to follow clients coming from your site. One vendor is permitted different associate connections and every one of them will guide the clients to its site. 12 One more methodology that works in subsidiary showcasing is the utilization of page codes or web treats. This is really an extremely fascinating method for stilling benefit regardless of whether your guest taps on the partner connection and doesn't buy from the dealer's site on the double. How does this function? The second a client taps on the connection, a treat is put away in his PC, showing that the person visited the trader's webpage and recording your page as the one that eluded him to that site. If, suppose a long time later, the client at last chooses to purchase something from the vendor's internet-based store and types the web address of the dealer straightforwardly into his program, the treats put away in his PC will in any case perceive the buy as a reference from your subsidiary connection, permitting you to get a pay from the shipper. Note that treats have lapse, so you should peruse the associate program's terms cautiously to check the life expectancy of these treats. The outcome of subsidiary advertising has additionally cleared the way for the ascent of numerous internet-based organizations, for example, Amazon.com, which currently has many partners.

2.Affiliate Marketing

Article promoting is an internet publicizing system utilized by numerous organizations to advertise their sites, items or administrations by composing short articles that are connected with their industry. It is the act of posting these watchwords zeroed in compositions on article partnership locales that have a decent readership following. These articles will then be disseminated and distributed in the commercial center. Many believe that article promoting is a fundamental component in any web showcasing system. These articles have the expectation of 13 giving data and amusement to online clients. Normally, these articles have an asset box or bio box that shows the references and contact data of the essayist's business. The asset box may likewise contain a connection back to the site that the writer is elevating to draw in the per users to visit that site. Articles that are well-informed and composed are normally delivered and appropriated for nothing for the business to acquire validity inside the market. Through these articles, a site or online business will actually want to draw in additional new clients. Web advertisers typically present the articles to a few article registries to boost the consequences of their internet-based crusade. To keep away from the sifting system of the web for copy content, web advertisers endeavor what we call text rewriting or article changing and revamping to give specific varieties to the first article. Through this, the article can get webpage guests coming from a few sites for article catalogs. Persuading your article to be highlighted in specialty writers or centered content sites that are overseen by others is a decent and famous procedure as far as article showcasing. In the event that you are a visitor blogger on these sites, you will actually want to acquaint yourself with an intrigued crowd that might have been generally inaccessible. The normal practice in web distribution is to have your articles utilize significant watchwords and appealing titles with around 250 to 500 words in the body. Assuming that you consolidate the watchwords or catchphrase phrases in your articles, it is possible to get more web search tool traffic. 14 Which, among the many article indexes, would it be advisable for you to present your articles to? This is really perhaps the most drawn-out task in this promoting strategy. Today, organizations and specialists typically rethink their article promoting strategies including the accommodation interaction. The most well-known article indexes that are suggested incorporate Ezine Articles, Idea Marketers and Go Articles.

Article Marketing

Article promoting can likewise assist you with creating drives that you can remember for your email list. As a hard copy of your articles, you should give the per users a deal so overwhelming that it will incite them to visit your site and pursue your administrations. When you have their data, you can begin making a deal winning organization with them. Neglecting to do this won't allow you one more opportunity to offer to your leads. Among the best offers you can give your per users might incorporate tests, unique reports on a specific subject, free discussion meetings or free book parts. Along these lines, your per users will be tempted to give you their email that you can use to additionally send promoting news and data about your site. By and large, the main figure article showcasing is to get individuals to visit your site and sign up or buy one of your administrations. Composing articles that are exact, explicit and accommodating will draw in additional possible leads or clients.

3.Email Marketing

This is one of the most expensive productive techniques for web advertising that advances your business. To execute a compelling and fruitful email crusade, you really want the right data to accomplish your ideal outcomes. Email showcasing is an immediate promoting technique that utilizes messages to convey a business message to your objective market. It is the most common way of sending messages to your past or current clients to urge them to work with you once more and thus upgrade your business relationship with them. Email showcasing is likewise used to secure new clients and persuade your ongoing clients to purchase something without a moment's delay. There are a few benefits in utilizing this sort of web promotion. As far as one might be concerned, practically all web clients have email accounts that they check routinely. With this type of correspondence, sponsors can undoubtedly arrive at the people who have joined to get normal interchanges in regards to subjects that intrigues them. It is practical and has a short effect time. Email advertising can be classified into three sorts: direct email, mediator email and maintenance email. 16 Direct messages for the most part is an email message with business deals content. They are typically shipped off clients who have recently utilized a specific item or administration or to likely clients in your interest group who could appreciate and profit from the help you are advertising. Post office-based mail showcasing may utilize an organization's email list or a bought or shared email list or a rundown that is procured from an outsider help. These outsider administrations may definitely know which crowd can be focused through email advertising or they might lead an investigation to figure out which email tends to bring the most elevated change or reactions for your business. Maintenance email or bulletin mail then again, are planned and composed for special use. They expect to give a drawn-out effect on the client's brain; consequently, their substance is in excess of a dead message. The maintenance mail determines the advantages of the items or administrations that an organization offers in a more educational configuration. Middle person email is a message sent by an organization designated by the principal supplier to convey publicizing and promoting messages to a rundown of endorsers that is typically claimed by the delegate organization. To find success in email promoting, you should continuously utilize all pertinent data that is vital for your business. You might send messages to your clients assuming you find that they will profit from what you are going to offer them. In sending these messages, you should likewise compose a useful and straight forward title 17 to catch your client's eye. Prior to conveying your email, check the message and utilize both message and HTML configurations to ensure that your message will be gotten and perused, or you might incorporate choices to see your mail in these arrangements.

4.Blog Marketing

Sites have become one of the valuable stages for web promotion. Supporters of a blog typically join to get content consistently and since most endorsers stay steadfast when they get important and helpful data, a solid following and readership will be an effective method for arriving at these likely clients and inspire them to one or the other sign up or buy an assistance from your business. Online journals have constantly arrived at their objectives more often than not, making them an extremely compelling method for showcasing one's administrations or items. Blog promoting, as the name proposes, is done by means of a web blog through a progression of week by week or everyday posts about a specific point. A ton of organizations have utilized websites to impart and interface with their clients while highlighting their administrations. Associations have likewise utilized web journals to share and survey an item's highlights and advantages preceding their authority send off. They likewise clear ways for organizations to assemble or get criticism from the buyers to affirm assuming their administrations and items live up to the assumptions of their clients. 18 Since blog promotion centers around collaboration with online clients, you may likewise begin publishing content to a blog to showcase your product offering to get more openness to the digital market. Nonetheless, you should compose and plan a blog that will stand apart from your rivals. Along these lines, your blog will likewise acquire prevalence, making more sites need to connect to it. The more sites connecting to your blog, the more traffic and benefit you will get. You should constantly make sure to convince your crowd or target endorsers to consistently visit your blog. On the off chance that your supporter leaves any remarks, make certain to send them a thank you email. Hold little challenges once in a while where you can offer limits and coupons to your endorsers. You may likewise request that your devotees post the connection of your blog to their own sites in return with the expectation of complimentary item tests.

5. Pay-per-click or PPC

Pay-per-click commercials, otherwise called Cost Per Snap, are accustomed to acquire traffic to sites where sponsors give pay to the facilitating site at whatever point their promotion is clicked. There are two models for deciding how much is to be paid per click - level rate and bid-based rate. In the two models, publicists consider the worth of a tick from a specific source where such worth relies upon the sort of client that the organization is focusing on and what can be acquired from their visit (which is generally income). 19 In the event that you as of now have a running site or a blog and might want to procure additional benefit, you can attempt this web promoting technique. Put in pay-per-click promotions on your blog or website page and vendors will pay you a rate each time your guests click on them. One of the most well-known PPC is Google AdSense. It is extremely simple to add this to your blog and that's only the tip of the iceberg so assuming you use Blogger which is likewise overseen by Google. AdSense shows various commercials that focus on a particular crowd on your blog. To pursue pay-per-click promotions like Google AdSense, you should finish a web-based structure as your authority application.

6. Search Engine Optimization

(Web optimization) At whatever point you look for a subject on Google, Hurray or MSN, you as a rule get endless pages of sites that have the watchwords you composed in the pursuit bar. Have you at any point asked why a specific site is recorded first on the consequences of your inquiry? The essential justification behind this is Website improvement. Site improvement permits a site to become a web search tool cordial, making it rank higher on indexed lists contrasted with different sites that have similar catchphrase contents. Normally, these web search tools read and document locales consistently with the goal that they can be found effectively at whatever point a pursuit is performed by a client. For instance, on the off chance that a client types in "nurturing" in the hunt bar and your site is about a similar subject and is streamlined appropriately, your site will show up in the principal page of the query items. 20 Essentially, Web optimization makes your site more straightforward for these web search tools to comprehend. It will likely expand your site's position in the query items that will thus acquire more traffic to your site. Keep in mind, the more traffic you get, the more potential revenue driven you will have. On location and off-site factors are the ones that can decide your web search tool rankings. On location factors incorporate your page content and your title heading. Off-site factors like pages that connect to your site, words used to connect to your page and how lengthy such connection has existed additionally become possibly the most important factor. You actually must zero in on your site's Website design enhancement constantly since, supposing that you get great web crawler rankings reliably, you will continuously have free traffic.

7.Pop-Up Ads

During your web riding time, you presumably have gone over large numbers of these spring up advertisements. These are ad windows that show up once you visit a site. Their point is to create traffic or straightforward catch your email address. Many individuals have found this web showcasing strategy very irritating since it upsets them from getting data from the site they are seeing. In any case, these advertisements, nosy as they have been labeled, additionally enjoy specific benefits. For one's purposes, they are substantially more compelling than flag advertisements. They get up a 15% active visitor clicking percentage while the standards just yield a simple 3%. Spring up promotions likewise are compelling and give a navigate 21 level of 6.5. Since they are more viable than flag promotions, they likewise set you back much more. Notwithstanding, the profit from ventures with the utilization of these advertisements is a lot higher. Moreover, when this promotion is the main window on the page, there will be no different pictures that will struggle with the brand that you are selling. In the new year's however, these promoting strategies have become less famous because of the improvement of spring up blockers.

8. Banner Ads

A pennant promotion is essentially a realistic message or a picture shown on sites that mean to advance an organization's item or administration. They are little HTML codes, however their significance in web advertising and business is huge. Standard promotions change in sizes and direction yet will frequently come in rectangular shape and are 486 x 60 pixels high (full pennant). There is no general rule with regards to flag promotion document sizes, yet the size will in any case rely upon the site where it will be shown. These locales force specific cutoff points to standard sizes since it amounts to the all-out size of the site page they are shown on, in this manner coming about to additional holding up times while the page loads on a program. Because of the pennant promotions' realistic components, you might find these advertisements some way or another like those you see in printed media like magazines and papers. Notwithstanding, these pennant promotions can guide the client to the sponsor's fundamental website page. In the event that you are keen on showing or posting a standard on a specific site, you can organize with the 22 distributors to have your flag posted or pay a pennant organization to post the promotion on various sites. You may likewise organize with the distributor to just show their advertisements on your site in return for them showing your standard promotions.

9. Social Media Marketing

Web-based entertainment promotion is essentially the most common way of advertising your business through online entertainment gateways like Facebook, YouTube and Twitter. This takes into consideration organizations to have a more private and dynamic communication and association with their clients and possible clients. Techniques in web-based entertainment showcasing can be basically as straightforward as keeping a blog, a Facebook or Twitter account or connecting "tweet this" symbols to the furthest limit of your articles or promotions. It can likewise be basically as perplexing as having a full mission that incorporates writing for a blog, interpersonal interaction, tweeting and spreading viral recordings. As promoting is the most common way of illuminating purchasers what your business is, what your identity is and what your items are, online entertainment further aids in acquainting your business with a worldwide organization of potential clients. The utilization of online entertainment to demonstrate a business' character and to make business associations with individuals who don't get the opportunity to know about your items and administrations is a strongly suggested choice in web promoting. In addition, a road can be gotten to by anybody who has a web 23 association and is a modest method for executing your showcasing techniques and business crusades.

10. Mobile Marketing

Portable promoting has been an idea that has accomplished different definitions. It is essentially portrayed to be the promoting system that utilizes versatile media to speak with an objective market. As of late a more refreshed definition was given by the Versatile Promoting Affiliation, saying that portable showcasing is really a blend of practices that enables associations to draw in, impart and collaborate with their crowd through a cell phone or organization. The most well-known cell phone utilized for this is a PDA. To utilize this medium, you should set up a short code and have your clients register to accept your SMS or instant messages. Versatile improvement will likewise ensure that your site is shown accurately on a cell phone program. Site improvement has gone through many changes that caused web advertisers to turn out to be keener on the portable variant of their advanced sites contrasted with the customary site streamlining. Most cell phones today have web access or remote abilities. These gadgets have given greater adaptability on both the business' and shopper's finishes as far as getting and sending information connected with the items or administrations which an organization offers. 24 The most average sorts of versatile promoting incorporate the utilization of MMS or Media Informing Administration, Bluetooth innovation, Infrared and Portable Web. Showcasing through a cell phone is currently a pattern in many created nations where nearly everybody has a cell phone. This is likewise a more financially savvy technique for advancing your business and is a lot simpler for most age gatherings to comprehend. Additional time is presently spent online with the utilization of these gadgets, making your business accessible to shoppers who are generally in a hurry and would in any case need to get refreshes from your end. In MMS portable showcasing, a slideshow of text and pictures that might incorporate a video or sound is an ideal method for catching a potential client's consideration. The promotion is conveyed through MMS. The utilization of Bluetooth innovation in showcasing utilizes radio-put together frequencies to move information with respect to higher velocities. Infrared, then again, is a piece restricted, as its recurrence range just reaches similar to 1 meter. Versatile showcasing is a better approach to guarantee client mindfulness and lift your deals. With every one of the new advanced cells, tablets and current cell phones, versatile advertising is most certainly bound to advance in the years to come. All the significant web promoting techniques have been talked about exhaustively in this aid. It is presently dependent upon you to pick which one you like, nonetheless, recall the things that you want to have to succeed - great exploration, a positive outlook and demeanor, steadiness, persistence and concentration. The very best.

ABOUT THE AUTHOR

Isah Abdulwali Garba

Is an expert when it comes to making money online.

He is a final year student of Abubakar Tafawa Balewa University Bauchi (ATBU).

What makes this book unique is that everything inside is from personal experience.

www.ingramcontent.com/pod-product-compliance
Lightning Source LLC
Chambersburg PA
CBHW071130220526
45467CB00004B/2095